T0017546

I've never met anyone who does not struggle with self-discipline. The problem with self-discipline is usually identified as a lack of willpower, a lack of follow through. You commit to a program, with every good intention, and wake up a few days later having "failed."

A few of us are on the other side of the continuum, so disciplined we "fail" at things like kindness, spontaneity, and relaxation. One way or another, the struggle to be disciplined takes a lot of energy, often misspent. There is a convoluted belief about self-discipline that many of us have taken on:

THE BELIEF

"If I were different—better, smarter, thinner, richer, more in control (which I would be if only I had more self-discipline!) life would be as it should be and I would be happy. As it is, life isn't the way it should be and it's my fault."

I contend that what we think of as the problem with self-discipline is not the problem at all, and the solutions we try, sincere as they are, lead only to frustration and failure. So, as I see it, this belief is not true.

- Nothing in life is a matter of "fault,"

- no amount of self-discipline will ever give anyone control over life (control is an illusion),

- happiness does not depend on circumstances,

- and life is always exactly as it is.

There are two kinds of self-discipline.

1. Strict, harsh, and punishing

Do not give in to weakness.

Push ahead no matter what.

your lack of resolve is pathetic.

You're a failure if you quit.

2. Supported, assisted, and nurtured

I will not abandon myself no matter what.

I will ask for help if I need it.

Deep down this is what I really want.

I know I cannot fail if I do this with love.

The first is familiar to us all.

The second,
compassionate self-discipline,
is nothing other than being present
rather than engaged in
distracted, unfocused, addictive
behaviors based in an
I-need-to-fix-myself mentality.

That person is actually paying attention,
focusing on what is here to do in this
moment, bringing compassion to all
aspects of daily life, and discipline has
nothing to do with it.

We don't lack self-discipline,
we lack presence.

Compassionate self-discipline
is simply allowing
the intelligence and generosity
that is your authentic nature
to guide you in every moment.

With this guidance you will be not only
disciplined, you will be spontaneous, clear,
awake, aware, efficient, appropriate,
respectful, grateful, kind, honest,
sincere, expressive, steady, dependable,
responsible, peaceful, joyful, and
satisfied.

These are only a few descriptions of the
experience.

Discovering compassionate self-discipline
may be easier, and harder,
than you thought.

On the one hand,
it is not necessary
to come up with more
sophisticated methods
for making your "self"
do what your self does not want to do.
No more planning, hoping, fearing, and
failing.

On the other hand,
you will need to choose
in-the-moment presence
over the habitual patterns of a
"conditioned mind."

CONDITIONED MIND

The everyday mind through which we interact with life is the result of a system of brainwashing called "socialization." From the first moment of life a child is taught what is right, wrong, ugly, beautiful, sacred, worldly, important, valuable, worthless; who the right people are, which values are important, which god to believe in, what heaven is, what hell is, how a person should be, how others should be, how the world should be, how people should be punished, what it means to be a man, what it means to be a woman...

In other words, every aspect of life has been programmed. (For most people, "going beyond" their childhood socialization is simply doing the opposite of what they were taught.) This program - whether adhering to it or rebelling against it - is what we call conditioned mind.

Everything you have attempted
for as long as you can remember
has been under the direction
of a socially and karmically
conditioned mind.

Every conditioned human being is in a constant, primary relationship with a voice in their head telling them, second by second, what is so, real, true, right, good, beautiful, worthwhile, important, and desirable, as well as what is wrong, bad, to be avoided, unpleasant, ugly, and so on.

The voice lets them know how they feel and if they're being the right person.

It scans for what's wrong and points out mistakes.

Whoa!!
No way!!
Foul!!
Wrong, wrong, wrong, wrong, wrong!!

In other words, it creates and maintains the reality of each individual.

As you read this, the process I'm describing is going on. Conditioned mind is taking this in and looking to see if the information is true. Perhaps it's beginning to argue, "Do I agree with this? I don't have a voice in my head pointing out that stuff to me second by second."

That's it! That's the voice.

Casual observation will show that you are constantly looking somewhere to get the information you're getting about every aspect of life. For instance, you decide to learn a new skill.

The decision, the approach, the beliefs about your abilities, success, failure, and so forth arise in conditioned mind. You may be aware of voices of enthusiasm or trepidation, and you may hear negative, even punishing voices saying you can't succeed because you have some built-in flaw that will prevent success. As you proceed, you are constantly following the directions, assumptions, and assessments coming from conditioned mind. You look to conditioned mind to tell you how you're doing. Depending on the response you get, you will feel good or bad. Are you learning this new skill quickly and easily? You get to feel good, proud, pleased. Are you learning it faster than others? Better still. Not meeting the standards? Oops. We know what that says about you.

Conditioned mind is framing your life, and in this book we are going to turn the tables on it.

Rather than "it" being in charge, calling the shots, making the decisions about what you do and how you feel, "you" will have the opportunity to observe "it" and to realize that you can have your own present moment experience of life. You will have a chance to be in life without the filter of conditioning.

So the question is not
"How do I become
more disciplined?"

The question is
"How do I learn to live
in the present?"

EXERCISE

What does "self-discipline" mean to you?

What is your history with self-discipline?

What assumptions do you have about
self-discipline?

2. Who's Talking?

Perhaps the greatest help in introspective work is sorting out "who the players are," who is talking, and who is listening.

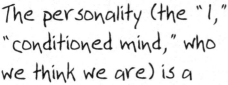

The personality (the "I," "conditioned mind," who we think we are) is a composite of many parts, many aspects of the personality. Aspects of the personality are survival strategies we developed to make it through childhood. When you were being taught to fit into society—when you were being "socialized" —you concluded that you were the cause of other people's unhappiness, that there was something wrong with you, and that you needed to be different. You threw temper tantrums when you were two and three and they got you a lot of what you wanted. By the time you were four, that wasn't working anymore so you became a "performer" or a "helper," or you withdrew or rebelled, or you adapted in a way that, to your child's mind, seemed like it would be acceptable to those around you, get your needs met, and ensure your survival.

A new aspect of the personality was "born" each time you needed to adapt throughout your early years.

Now, as an adult, those aspects of you are still operating. Sometimes you're talkative, other times withdrawn; sometimes charming, cautious, irritable, obsessed by a project; a procrastinator— the list is long for most people. We learn to recognize aspects of the personality by paying attention to what they say. They are many of "the voices in your head."

For me, there is a student of Zen, a teacher, a writer, an athlete, a philosopher, an engineer, a psychologist, a mother, a daughter, a grandmother, a sister, a best friend, someone who is stubborn and tenacious, a soft-hearted marshmallow, an animal lover, a quick temper, a crusader rabbit, a champion of the underdog, and many more.

EXERCISE

Imagine going through an average day.

"Who" wakes up in the morning? (Who picks out your sleepwear?) Who decides what to do first? Is someone in charge of the morning rituals? Who fixes breakfast? (Sometimes it might be the "health food fascist," sometimes the "junk food junkie.") Who decides what to wear? Is there someone who plans your day? Who makes lists? Who rehearses beforehand? Who goes to work? Take time and consider that this might be a whole crew of "people," depending on circumstances. Who plans your evening? Do you have a daydreamer, a fantasizer, a romantic, a veg-out-in-front-of-the-TV-with-beer-and-pizza? Who else?

Again, aspects of the personality form to help us adjust to the ever-changing demands from those raising us. We were not acceptable as we were so we modified ourselves to get by. In my family it didn't work to be softhearted so I became mean and prickly to protect myself. Only after I found the safety of center was that soft-heartened person allowed to be a major player in my life.

CENTER

Center is the unconditionally accepting, conscious, compassionate awareness that is our authentic nature. It is the nonseparate reality that contains, and is able to embrace, the illusion of a separate self, called "I," "me," "my," that suffers. When in center, everything is as it is and none of it is taken personally. There is nothing wrong; no loss, lack, or deprivation; no fear; no urgency. The feeling of center is often described as peaceful, compassionate, energetic, willing, and joyful. From center, the world is exactly the same as always, there's just nothing wrong.

In my experience, aspects of the personality are feelings combined with beliefs and behaviors. The "responsible" aspect of me has beliefs about what being responsible is, acts the way it thinks it should, feels good or bad depending on meeting or not meeting standards, and

PROJECTION

When we look out at the world, we do not see the world as it is, we see the world as we are. The only thing we ever experience is ourselves. The world is simply a mirror. Simply put, if you are in a wonderful mood, if you've just fallen in love, the world is a glorious place full of beauty and promise. If you are miserable, if you just lost a pile of money in the stock market, the world is a hateful, hopeless, unfair place in which nothing good will ever happen for you. The world did not change.

projects like crazy onto me and everyone else.

All aspects of the personality refer to themselves as "I". As you attend closely, you can hear them talk back and forth...

about you!

Because aspects of the personality are there to meet specific needs, they are single-focused. The part that makes a commitment is not the same part that breaks it. They are two different aspects. Each is there to take care of you in a particular way. Once a need is met, that aspect of the personality disappears and the next need arises, along with the aspect of the personality charged with meeting that need. (Keep in mind that not all needs being met are supportive of the person.)

While aspects of the personality may appear to be any age, emotionally they are rarely older than three or four years. They wreak havoc in our lives, demanding that we meet their needs and all the "adult" versions of those desires, but children they are. Each was created to meet a need when we were too young to do anything but adapt and survive.

They aren't bad,
can't be gotten rid of,
and when embraced and appreciated
become delightful companions.

They want stuff all the time.
They're rambunctious,
frightened,
exuberant,
thoughtless,
adorable,
and utterly selfish.

They are meet-my-needs machines.
And, they're yours.
Lucky you.

I mean that "lucky you" part.

Getting to know the complex set of
characters that compose "me" allows you
to become more aware of why self-
discipline may be a challenge. As you get
to know the aspects of the personality,

you are able to call forth the aspect that makes and keeps commitments, that loves a project, and that delights in learning new things.

Once you establish yourself as the conscious, compassionate presence, your fun quotient will go through the roof.

EXERCISE

List some of the aspects of your personality and what they say. For example, which part of you says:

"I don't have time."
"I should have known better."
"I'll probably fail."
"I want to meditate."
"Don't tell me what to do."

Add your own:

3. Meditation

In meditation we practice presence, fully present to our experience, to see through the delusions of conditioned mind and end suffering.

SUFFERING

Pain is an inevitable part of being alive and in physical form. Suffering results from resisting pain, from wanting something other than what is. Suffering can be anything from abject grief to irritation at the traffic. Probably the best synonym for suffering is dissatisfaction. We suffer when we resist what is.

Meditation is a technique for getting HERE. Conditioned mind is a process of, as well as a result of, habitual distraction. Attention flits from thing to thing to thing—thoughts, sensations in the body, emotions, memories, plans, colors, lights, conversations—only briefly passing through here/now.

Life happens here/now.
Everything other than
here/now is illusion.

The constant pull away from conscious awareness of one's time and place in the present maintains the delusion of other, optional, parallel realities.

Meditation has been practiced throughout the world for thousands of years. In cultures where meditation has been an integral aspect of life, practitioners have learned that sitting in a certain posture—spine straight, body relaxed—is most conducive to being present. Sitting in this position minimizes physical pain and sleepiness.

A Meditation Posture

Sit on the first one-third of the meditation cushion. If you sit on a meditation bench,  stool, or chair, sit well forward. Adjust your leg position until you find one that you can maintain comfortably. Straighten your posture by pushing up from the base of the spine. Imagine that you are trying to touch the ceiling with the crown of your head. As you do this, the chin will tuck slightly and the pelvis will 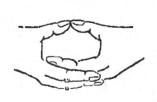 tilt slightly forward. The shoulders and abdomen relax. The eyes are open and unfocused, lowered, and looking at the wall or floor at a 45-degree angle. The hands are in the cosmic mudra. The right hand is positioned a few inches below the navel, palm up. The left hand, also palm up, rests inside the right hand. The tips of the thumbs touch lightly, forming an oval.

The Breath

To stay present and alert in meditation, it can be helpful to focus on the breath. As you sit, breathe naturally and normally. On the first exhalation silently count 1; on the next, count 2; continue until you reach 10; start over at 1. If your attention wanders, gently bring it back and begin again at 1.

Sit for up to 30 minutes. Meditation is not a contest. Being present with yourself for 5 minutes will be much more helpful than 30 minutes on a cushion with conditioned mind beating you up for whatever you are doing wrong or have forgotten to do. If your choice is between a kind meditation and a long one, choose the kind one.

Everything will arise in a meditation practice. If two aspects of you are equally committed

to "yes" and "no," you can get into an arm-wrestling contest over meditation. As you practice you will see if the part of you saying "no" really doesn't care about meditation but simply wants you to fail. You will also see if the part that says "yes" really does want to meditate or is just attempting to "be the right person."

In meditation you will encounter the conditioning that has been in control of your life. It's not going to say, "Oh, you don't want to suffer anymore? You want to be in charge of your life? You don't want me to make you miserable? OK, no problem." Au contraire! It will fight you tooth and nail. Those voices that you always believed were who you are, the ones accustomed to being in control, are going to start campaigning against this meditation stuff. My encouragement is don't give up. You CAN outlast them. As difficult as it might be to believe when the voices are loudly complaining, your resources are greater. Make a commitment to meditation or anything else, follow through, have something come up to interfere, break your commitment, and commit again! When we're simply present to the whole process, "failure" and "lack of self-discipline" are beside the point. Letting yourself down is beside the point. Being disappointed is beside the point. Feeling discouraged is beside the point. Those reactions are designed to stop you. Recommitting is the point.

If you get talked into quitting, when you wake up, when you remember who you are, get right back to conscious, compassionate awareness. Don't let those voices use awareness against you. If you hear, "Look at you. You quit! You'll never get this. Look how long you've been trying to be aware and you're still a failure at it," realize this is conditioned mind trying to control you, and recommit.

If you pay close attention, you will see how a process has been keeping you prisoner. You're going to learn that when you're present in the moment you don't need to fear yourself, anyone, or anything.

> A huge part of doing this work
> is getting to the point
> where it all falls apart.

We don't need to know how to get through the good times! We need to learn what to do when things don't go well, when the voices get the better of us, when we feel like a failure and want to give up. What I hear over and over is that people start something they want to do, do whatever it is, feel great, stop (for reasons they rarely understand), and get the stuffin' beat out of them by conditioned voices for being a loser and a failure. It's a cycle. It's the universal condition of conditioned humans. The whole thing is designed to go to the point of failure. The whole thing is set up to get to the beating. We are going to see through that, eliminate the beating, and be free of the whole cycle.

Good deal, huh? You'll stop living in fear that if you're successful and feel good about yourself you'll set off an avalanche of self-hatred. You will stop living small in an attempt to avoid beatings.

Conditioned mind will try to convince you it is too painful to face your suffering, and it will try to make you believe it is too painful to face the suffering in the world. Facing suffering, embracing suffering, being the conscious, compassionate awareness that can bring an end to suffering is not painful. Trying to hide from suffering is painful and will rob you of your life.

At some point we must,
without self-hatred,
stand at the crossroads,
hear the little voice that says
"You can go in a new direction,"
heed that voice,
and make a choice to end suffering.

Fortunately,
we are at the crossroads
in each moment,
and the gentle urging
is always with us.

The choice is clear: You can muddle along through life following the voices of conditioning as they lead you to more feeling bad, or you can step free of them and be your own person. You can live from center.

I'm encouraging you to find 5 minutes in your day that you could devote to awareness practice,
meditation,
contemplation,
to something that will
lead you to the clear
vision of who you are
that you're yearning for.

We have plenty of time and willingness. We're spending our time on what we're currently spending it on, and we're willing for what we currently have in our lives. We need to check in with exactly how we're spending our time and what it is we're willing for.

A woman told me that each morning she gets up to let her dogs out into the yard for their morning constitutional.

She doesn't want to waste time while they're outside so she checks her email. While she's waiting for her laptop to boot up, she plays a game or two or ten of solitaire, whatever she can get in before the dogs start barking.

My response? Thank goodness conditioned mind is helping you not waste time!!!

My suggestion? How about setting up a place from which it is possible to be sensitive to the dogs and away from the temptation of the computer? Find a chair, sit down, turn your attention to your breath, and notice what happens.

This is about as far away from a waste of time as a person can get!

Life is a tidal wave.

If you wait for things to calm down to start swimming with the current, you might not survive the wait.

Now is the time, and you are equal to the task.

Take the time you would waste listening to conditioned mind and put that time to good use. If you want to go deeper with this issue, you might decide on a time to get up each day for the next month and use that commitment in the 30-day program at the end of this book. It doesn't have to be the same time every day; it could be one time during workdays and another for days off. It could be a different time every day.

It doesn't matter what time you set, only that you do what you've committed to.

4. Disidentification

I want to do something.
I do it.
I feel good.
Voices talk me out of doing it.
The same voices beat me up for quitting.

I'll bet all of us can see ourselves in that progression. After the beating (or during) comes the conclusion that what I do or don't do says something about who and how I am. If I don't go to the gym I'm lazy, a slug, an undisciplined loser,  hopeless, useless, and headed for an ugly death. Seeing that having those kinds of thoughts is a process, is a pattern, rather than believing the content of the thoughts is true, creates a distance, disidentification, and from that larger perspective, I begin to question the veracity of what I'm being told.

We're learning to accept ourselves exactly as we are. Seeing and accepting ourselves require us to "disidentify" from conditioned mind.

DISIDENTIFICATION
(WHEW!)

Disidentification is stepping back, creating a distance so that we can watch conditioned mind instead of being caught in it and believing it. For example, I've decided to begin a meditation practice. As I consider that, I recall how many times I've made that decision and failed. I'm just not a disciplined person. When I stay inside my head with this conversation, it seems like it's just "me" thinking. When I step back and observe the process, I realize conditioned mind is telling me who and how I am and what is possible for me. With this disidentification, I can recognize the voice of conditioning and that IT is talking to "ME." Disidentification is moving from identification with conditioning to observing conditioning.

As we watch conditioning, we begin to see how we got stuck in certain places in life and how we still get stuck. As we pay attention, we stop believing the **content** of life - family, money, health, work (endless list), and focus on the internal **processes** that maintain our struggles.

HOW do I suffer?
HOW do I stay stuck?
HOW do I wind up in the same place?

CONTENT & PROCESS

CONTENT: The "whats," stuff, issues, problems - the furniture of your life. Job, money, relationship, family, health, possessions... - all content.

PROCESS: The "how," the way, the manner, the attitude of mind and heart.

EXAMPLES: Anxiety is a process. What I'm anxious about is the content. Love is a process. What/Who I love is the content.

Conditioned mind constantly directs our focus to the content.

For instance: My relationship problem is my partner. If only he/she/they would be different, I would be happy. How can I get my partner to change?

No, no, no! As you have doubtless noticed, that does not get you where you want to go. Better questions would be:

How do I put and keep my partner in the problem position?

What do I believe about relationship?

Which aspects of my personality are involved in the relationship?

What does each of them believe?

What am I projecting onto my partner?

In this practice, Job One is to see through the process that is keeping you from the life you know is available.

The content within that process can be anything. You might want to lose weight, start a meditation practice, stop yelling at the kids, be kinder to your partner, be on time, save money, exercise, keep the house tidier, be more pleasant, drive slower, eat healthier food, find a different job, stop worrying.

An example of the kind of process we are seeing and seeing through: You want to do something, you don't follow through, and you get called a failure with no willpower. Because of your lack of willpower, you can't be successful. But sometimes success happens in spite of the dire predictions of the voices, at which point sabotage kicks in. Soon you have failed once again. "See, I was right, I just can't do it."

Here is how the content might show up for that specific process. Say you want to be less irritable with your father. You lay out your plan for being the perfect, loving, understanding son. He starts in with his usual rant; you've had a hard day and lose patience. "See," a voice concludes, "you can't do it. You're weak. You have no resolve. You can't stick with anything. Give it up. You're a failure." If you have a successful time with your father, the voices take another tack: "Oh, sure you did OK this time, but just wait until next time. He'll point out what a disappointment you are, and you'll lose it just like you always do."

Perhaps your process is less specific: I know I would be happy if only I would (fill in the blank), but I don't stick with it, and so I'm hopeless, and it's all my fault that I'm unhappy.

My examples may not be exact for you, but I bet if you spend a little time looking you will identify the formula the voices use with you.

Once you see how it's done,
you will begin to recognize
that same process
with every piece
of content in your life.

HUGE freedom comes
when we can hear the voices and not
believe them. They have their faux
existence in a conditioned reality.
They are projecting.
They say what is true for them
and you believe it has something to do
with you.
It doesn't.

When we're present,
when we're disidentified,
we have a whole different relationship
with the voices.
It's when we're not present
and believing the voices,
that we suffer.

When we're caught by conditioning,
it's damned if you do, damned if you don't.

You're in an important meeting. If you
say something it was the wrong thing to
say or you didn't express yourself well. If
you don't speak up, you're the cause of
every wrong thing from that moment
forward.

You eat that piece of cake the voice is
telling you to eat, and you're called an
undisciplined pig as soon as you swallow
the last bite. If you don't eat the cake,

the voices will convince you that cake was
your last hope for happiness and you blew
the opportunity.

"Duality" holds suffering in place.

DUALITY

This conditioned reality we live in is called the world of opposites. No coin comes without two sides. There is no good without bad, beautiful without ugly, but our conditioning tells us there should be. We suffer when we cling to one side of a duality and reject the other. Acceptance transcends duality. Accepting that life is sometimes this, sometimes that, suffering falls away.

Two aspects of the personality get on opposite ends of a duality. They argue and compare while The Judge, as "referee," points out what's wrong with each of them and "you" for having anything to do with them.

Example:
One aspect of me wants to do something fun that another aspect of me says I

shouldn't. It could be anything, but let's use going away for the weekend for this example.

"I want to go.
I need a break," says one aspect. "It's irresponsible. I need to catch up on my work," says another. "You can't even make a simple decision," says The Judge.

When we step back and disidentify from these aspects of ourselves, and stop believing this kind of conversation has validity, we realize that what "I" am is the conscious, compassionate awareness that sees all of this as it happens. From that centered perspective, I can see that I am not limited to the two bad choices the voices are offering.

We learn to stop the torture by turning attention away from it and toward something else. For me that something else is the breath, the moment, here, where I am.

**If we meditated daily
and did a quick check-in with ourselves
at the end of the day,
conditioning would have
a very hard time
keeping us in bondage.**

A good technique for disidentifying:

If the voices are very strong, if you feel yourself shrinking and are considering giving up, get out pen and paper and write down everything the voices say to you. Everything. The voices would like you to believe you won't live that long! Naturally they want you to believe that so you won't do the exercise and prove to yourself that you can outlast them. Keep writing until the feelings dissipate. If they start again, write again. Here's the thing to keep in mind: The less we believe conditioning, by stepping back and seeing it for what it is, the freer we are.

The secret is watching the process, seeing how it all works, staying focused on awareness rather than being caught in "I should/I shouldn't." If I'm caught up in the story, believing any of it, trying to be different, I'm miserable. If all those things are going on and I'm just noticing, not believing, not taking it personally, I'm free.

**Keep in mind
that this is a process,
a practice.**

And please remember:

There is no way to appease conditioned mind. What you can practice is to withdraw attention from it, disidentify.

Moment by moment, bring attention to the breath.

Give the hateful voice no energy. As difficult as it is to imagine, it has no energy of its own. It has only the energy it can get from you through your participation and resistance. (Here's the place to use our nonviolent sit-in training. We sit down, be still, and notice.)

When we don't resist,
        fight,
            argue,
                or feel bad,

the system cannot maintain itself.

5. The Voices of Self-Hate

Someone said to me in an amazed tone of voice, "There are people, voices in my head, talking to me, who don't like me and are mean to me. How did I not notice that?" It is surprising, but in fact

How did I miss that for all these years?

SELF-HATE

most people don't notice the voices until they're pointed out.

It's been going on so long, we're so used to the voices, we accept them so unquestioningly, that it's a shock when we finally recognize them. The voices have been there since before we can remember, so it's just "me," just "reality." And saddest of all, we believe those mean things being said are true.

Once we hear the voices,
once we tune in and realize
what's going on,
the magnitude of the situation
is such that we can be mortified
that we missed it.

It is essential that we don't
waste time feeling bad.
PERIOD.

Feeling bad is a misdirection ploy that
self-hate uses, a primary way we're kept
from seeing
conditioned mind as
the real cause
behind "lack of will
power and self-
discipline."

As long as I am feeling bad, I am accepting the premise that there is something wrong with me that I need to fix or change.

When I believe the voices of self-hate, I am caught in a never-ending self-improvement cycle that ends with failing to keep a commitment which leads to (wait for it) feeling bad! Self-improvement doesn't work. Never has. Never will.

Feeling bad is self-hate
running a cruel scam.
It is never helpful.

When the survival system that helped you make it through childhood moved from protecting you to protecting itself, self-hate was born.

Self-hate is the voice that calls you names, threatens you, points out your flaws, tells you what other people think about you, instills fear, makes cases against you and others, and is, in every way, hate-filled.

It is

and

and will do anything to maintain its position of control.

And here is the most important thing to know about self-hate: It is not you!

EXERCISE

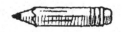

What does the voice of self-hate say to you and about you?

Do you believe what it says? If so, what does believing that voice bring to your life?

Can you consider not believing that voice? What would not believing it bring to your life?

Here is a quick look at self-hate in action:

You bought this book. You spent good money and went to some effort to obtain it because you want to have a different relationship with some things in your life. So, you get the book and start reading. This is all OK. (There is information in this book that conditioning will be able to use against you, so it has no problem

"USEFUL" INFO.

BLACKMAIL

THINGS SHE'LL FALL FOR

with you reading it.) But, suddenly, the tables are turning. You're being asked to look at conditioning itself. "Whoa! Wait a darn minute! I don't like this. I don't want to do this. This is stupid. This is a waste of time." Now, who do you think is talking? Your heart? Your authentic nature? The part of you who wants not to suffer? The part of you who wants to be free to enjoy life?

As you listen to the voice complaining and resisting, be aware that you are, in fact, listening.

You are not talking! A voice is making a case for not reading this book, and you are listening to it! It has fooled you in the past because you were not paying close enough attention to see that it was talking and you were listening. You thought "you" were "it."

Conditioning has as many ways to protect itself as there are people. I often hear things such as:
"It feels weird to admit that I hear voices."
"It feels wrong to divide myself into aspects of the personality."
"I feel sorry for those hateful voices."

Again, don't fall for it.

Those are scams self-hate runs to defend itself from being exposed as the

joy-stealing,

energy-draining,

life-robbing

trickster it is.

Do you know the expression, "One definition of insanity is doing the same thing over and over and expecting a different result"? If you want to do the same thing you've always done, if you want to continue believing what the voices tell you, you'll stay where you are.

You'll make a firm commitment to
lose weight,
stop smoking,
exercise,
go back to school,
(add your own),
and everything will go well...

for a while.

Eventually, the voices will start campaigning that

it's just all too hard!

And when the voices tell you to stop, you'll stop,

and then they will beat you for stopping!

You will do your best to be the right person, fail, and the voices will shame you:

You didn't meet the standard!

You can count on it.

We NOTICE all of this,
    but we don't BELIEVE any of it.

Believing and noticing are not the same thing. Believing the voices will result in doing the same thing and getting the same result. Noticing will enable you to see: Who gets grumpy? Who doesn't eat right? Who has physical problems? Who doesn't care? Who is invested in maintaining the status quo?

Paying attention enables you to see
how you get distracted,
how you get fooled,
how you end up in the same
suffering place
over and over.

It is important to become familiar with everything that goes on inside your head, but you don't need to get caught up in it.

It's like listening to propaganda spread by a corrupt government. You listen so you can know what they're up to. You don't listen so you can join in their game.

− The government said today that blah blah blah...

We listen and notice and watch and pay attention to the process of suffering so we can see how we are controlled, how we are stopped from doing what we want to do, how we are kept from being as we want to be.

Who are the players?
Who do they talk to?
What do they say?
What happens when we believe them?

We listen and watch and pay attention without needing to change anything.

We observe and write it all down
until the whole system
of conditioned suffering becomes
OBVIOUS and is no longer believable.

**Those voices will declare loudly
that they want to be happy
and at peace,
but don't fall for it.**

They may seem content for a short while,
but soon a story will start up about
what's wrong or missing. If you begin an
awareness practice, it won't take you long
to discover this for yourself.

6. Mentoring: Kind and Wise Support

In *There Is Nothing Wrong with You*, over several pages in an increasingly loud voice (larger print), I make the point that

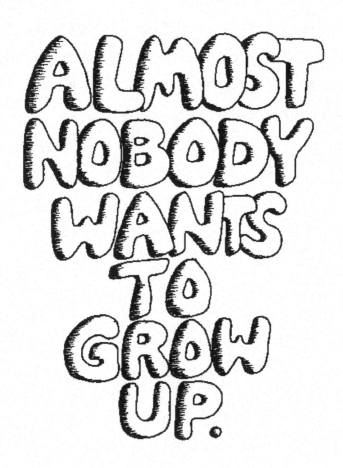

ALMOST NOBODY WANTS TO GROW UP.

In awareness practice "growing up" takes a whole new direction.

Not only will you be a grown-up in the sense of taking responsibility for yourself and your life, you will do it from consciousness and compassion. You will be "the Buddha," the awakened one, making centered choices in the moment, not stuck in conditioned reactions from the past.

This is a better approach to life than the ever-popular strategy of manipulating someone else into taking care of you.

It is my theory that until we learn to take care of ourselves, our lives are in the hands of egocentric karmic conditioning/self-hate.

Egocentric karmic conditioning/self-hate is another phrase we use to refer to the voices in conditioned mind.

EGOCENTRIC KARMIC CONDITIONING/SELF-HATE

Here are some synonyms for egocentric karmic conditioning/self-hate: the illusion of a self that is separate from the rest of life; that illusion's survival system; center-of-the-universe-ness; I as subject, everything else as object. Example: I drink coffee every morning because I saw my parents do it. I'm "karmically predisposed" to drink coffee because I'm conditioned to follow cultural norms. I have an identity as a coffee drinker. "The right people drink coffee." "Coffee connects people." "(Add your own.)" With this, I have slipped into the egocentric. What I do, how I am, how I see it is the right/good/acceptable way.

We'd all like to have someone who thinks we're wonderful,
encourages us,
and loves us unconditionally.

The good news is that we can be that compassionate presence for ourselves rather than seek it outside. Each of us has a Mentor within that is kind, perennially available, and unfailingly interested in our lives.

The Mentor I'm encouraging you to find is not a source of permissive self-indulgence. Nor is the Mentor a hard taskmaster who makes you do stuff you don't want to do "for your own good."

The Mentor speaks from conscious, compassionate awareness.
The Mentor, being center, loves you and all life unconditionally.

RECORDING AND LISTENING

We access the Mentor through a
Recording and Listening Practice—R/L,
for short.

Recording and Listening is the practice of
engaging with the Wisdom, Love and
Compassion that is our Authentic Nature.
Instead of living in relationship with the
voices of self-hate that are hell-bent on
only reinforcing what's wrong with us,
that drive us into never ending cycles of
self-improvement, failure and self-hate,
we can choose to go through life in the
friendly companionship of the Mentor
within.

**Compassionate self-discipline is
possible when the Mentor,
rather that egocentric karmic
conditioning/self-hate,
is our life coach.**

We have several books on R/L practice and an entire website dedicated to exploring this powerful tool. Since this book is about compassionate self-discipline, here are a few tips on how to use R/L practice in the context of making a change for good.

1. As we said in the introduction, we don't lack self-discipline, we lack presence. The R/L practice is a wonderful way to come back to presence. When you are attending to those voices in the head, you are not here. Picking up the recorder and talking about what's here, now, in your immediate awareness—birdsong, the feeling of your feet on the ground, the warmth of the breath,—brings you back to presence.

2. R/L practice is a powerful tool of disidentification. When you find yourself upset, discouraged or dissatisfied turn on the recorder and talk as you would to

your best friend (the Mentor) about what's going on for you. This allows the attention to move from listening to the voices harangue you to awareness that you were listening to voices harangue you. You are training to pay attention, notice the voices and not get identified with what they are saying.

3. The voices of self-hate are always angling to make you feel bad. Focusing the attention on what's wrong with you ensures the cycle of self-improvement will continue. R/L is a great antidote to self-hate. When self-hating voices begin their diatribe, listen to your recordings as a way to interrupt the programming. Your recordings can be about what you love, what is true for you, what is working, what's beautiful in your surroundings, what you are grateful for, how you want to be with yourself as you make and keep a commitment, your favorite songs and poems, the things that

light you up..., the list is endless! Rather than live in the small, unhappy world of conditioned mind, you can choose to live in a world as seen by the expansive lens of conscious awareness.

4. R/L is also a way to look at the process rather than to get mired in the content. As you talk to the Mentor about the content of your life and listen back to the recordings, you will see the beliefs and assumptions, the projections, the dualities, the self-hate..., all of the aspects of conditioning at play in your life. As you move from being caught in the content to watching the process, you are also disidentifying! From a disidentified perspective, you can see how not keeping commitments happens for you. From that clarity, you have the choice not to be controlled by conditioning.

5. The self-discipline to practice is compassionate self-discipline. As you

embark on a process of making a change for good, you can choose to do so in the companionship of your ideal friend or partner, the Mentor. The Mentor can be appreciative of your efforts, understanding of your "failures," provide wise counsel when you have set-backs and celebrate your accomplishments. Switch on the recorder and let the Mentor talk to you. You will be amazed at how accurately the Mentor can read your heart and offer what you need in the moment.

The relationship with the Mentor is like any other relationship: we make it strong in the easy times so it can sustain us through the hard times. Practice will make all the difference.

Egocentric karmic conditioning/self-hate has no interest in mentoring and will resist this practice mightily. But when it does, you can pick up the recorder, and

get HERE.
When you're HERE,
you're with the Mentor.

When you're HERE, with the Mentor, you
are in the presence of what has your
best interest at heart.

When you're HERE, with
the Mentor, you are the
grown-up that can assist
you to take care of
yourself.

7. Self-Discipline and Eating

Eating is often a source of great suffering. What and how much to eat are questions we face every day. If we are conscious, there is no problem. At a retreat a woman said, "I've noticed that I can generally maintain my commitment to lose a few extra pounds as long as I maintain conscious awareness while eating." This is a huge piece of the puzzle.

"Going unconscious" is the reaction to specific triggers. Rising energy that gets labeled "tension" is one of those triggers. A series of connections begins that takes the unaware person down a path of bad decisions. For instance, I am conditioned to ignore early warning signs of hunger. I'm busy, I'm involved in something important, and I avoid signals of growling stomach and dropping blood sugar. I can never remember to bring a snack or to avoid coffee and sugar when I won't be able to eat for several hours. Soon I am miserable. Inside I'm hysterical. I can't focus or concentrate. I hate everyone around me. When I finally get to food, I stuff myself with the quickest, easiest items I can get my hands on. I pack in way too many empty calories before my brain gets information about how much I've ingested. Alas, fast food is designed for the person in my condition. Snack foods are made for people in blood sugar crisis.

So, we want to bring conscious, compassionate awareness to the issue of food.

Someone, probably someone who rarely gets what she or he needs (a diet that feels good), wants to bring consciousness to a suffering relationship with food. Let's say the person who came up with this decision to be more conscious doesn't want to eat junk food. Now, this is not an unreasonable desire, wanting not to eat things that just about everyone except those selling the junk agrees is not good for you. It is not unreasonable to want support in being healthier.

But another someone (egocentric karmic conditioning/self-hate) is threatened by this desire. Why would that be so?

Because eating, along with every addiction we struggle with, is not about the content, it is about the process, and the process is "identity maintenance."

Who would I be if I had a kind, compassionate relationship with food? What would happen to self-hatred if I ate what was good for me and was healthy and felt good about myself? There would be no drama! There would be no suffering. There would be no egocentric karmic conditioning/self-hate to control me. And egocentric karmic conditioning/self-hate is not going to give up without a fight!

So, now that the fight is on, rules and willpower and forcing and "denying myself" are introduced. It can no longer be a simple matter of a decision not to eat junk food. It's a contest in which "I" will "make myself do what I don't want to do." But who is this "myself"? This is not the person who wants to feel better through avoiding junk food. Suddenly the desire to eat healthy food has become a matter of failure and screwing up and feeling bad. Who is the "I" behind this? It is egocentric karmic conditioning/self-hate turning eating well and feeling good into failure and misery.

Picture this: You have a friend who is having health issues and suspects he would feel better not eating junk food. Could you be supportive? Would it need to be about punishment and misery and deprivation and poor me? Of course not. If that were someone you loved, you would be coming up with healthy recipes, finding restaurants that serve delicious, nutritious choices, and encouraging tasty, healthy snacks.

The secret is to disidentify from the conditioning and start seeing ourselves as someone we love. When I no longer believe I need to or deserve to be beaten or mistreated or spoken to cruelly, I will stop believing the self-hating voices, and I will stop the behaviors that are not good for me. Overeating, eating junk, rewarding or punishing myself with food aren't compassionate—

and the unconscious behaviors are done precisely because they are not compassionate.

If you can stay conscious as the energy increases, if you can remain present to the sensations in your body rather than believing they mean you need to do something, you can sidestep the conditioned behaviors. That is a good argument for learning to pay close attention through the practice of meditation.

It's an even better argument for picking up the recorder and talking to the Mentor!

Conscious eating can be done in many ways. Here are a few:

- Put your fork down between bites.
- Bow between bites.
- Chew each bite 50 times.
- Chew 50 times, and then bow before taking another bite.
- Do not do anything other than eat while eating.

There are lots of fun variations.

You might hear voices beginning to grumble and complain. "This is too hard. This isn't any fun. It'll be boring." If you are tempted to believe them, make a recording in which you recall how little fun it is to overeat, to be overweight, to feel like an undisciplined failure, to listen to the voices going on about how you look and what it says about you that you have eating issues. Listen to the recording before you eat.

Here's the thing: If you love food, be present to eating. Smell the food. Look at it. Eat with your hands if you like so you can feel it. Take little bites and chew them a lot so you can savor every morsel. Make it last. Let it be sensual. Make it a feast, a feast for one, a party for you.

The voices want you to gobble your food without knowing what and how much you are eating, and then they want you to feel bad and dissatisfied afterward. Don't fall for it.

The easiest way for me to see compassionate self-discipline around food is to think of an adored child. I want that child to be happy, creative, spontaneous, free, adventuresome, and as safe as I can help her be. But, as with most children, as soon as she discovers sugar, it becomes the food group of choice. If I love that child I'm not going to let her eat sugar all day. She'd get sick. She'd be unhealthy. Loving that child means I'm going to take responsibility for showing up, being present, and offering the best food guidance I can. Perhaps a way of showing up would be to make a recording that reminds me of why I want to be present, available, conscious and aware in my approach to food; a recording that reminds me that I love this human being who wants to eat well and am willing to support and assist her.

Does this mean you will never again get to eat a piece of cake or candy? No, of course not. It means you will eat it when it is good for you to eat it, not when it's an unconscious decision from self-hate.

Let's say I commit to eating a limited amount of sugar once per day. I know sugar isn't good for me, I don't feel well, I weigh more than is comfortable, and I feel totally out of control with the issue.

Because I'm used to eating a lot of sugar every day, the stress is going to build. Voices start angling for their sugar. Conditioning starts distracting, making cases, dropping stupid dust, making deals.

STUPID DUST

Stupid dust is the illusion of confusion. Suddenly you can't remember what self-discipline is or why you ever thought it was a good idea or just exactly what is compassion anyway? It's a variation on the old "You are getting very sleepy..." as conditioning stupefies you and lulls you into unconsciousness. Even very intelligent people periodically get sprinkled with stupid dust.

Self-hate starts expressing an opinion about who and how I am for having an issue with sugar in the first place. I watch it all. I breathe and observe and record everything that goes on. By recording, I am practicing staying at center, disidentified, not drawn into the fray.

By talking to the Mentor, by attending to what the Wisdom, Love and Compassion has to say, I am practicing choosing compassion over conditioned voices of self-hatred. I'm taking responsibility for my health and well-being, and I'm doing it from the place that is most compassionate to all.

Compassion for the sugar addict,
compassion for the habit,
compassion for the body,
compassion for the opinions,
compassion for the person who wants to be free of the addiction.

8. Self-Discipline and Time Management

How do you apply
compassionate self-discipline
to time management?

Time management can include
punctuality,
use of time,
ability to focus,
distraction,
setting priorities,
organization...
add your own.

Perhaps you are a person who is always punctual. Perhaps that trait is in the category of "how people should be" and you feel good about it. We're taught to believe there is no reason to pay attention to areas in which we are doing well.

But in this practice we are focused on ending suffering, so I would ask you to consider the effect punctuality has on your life, and I don't mean only your punctuality.

Yes, you feel right and like a good person for being on time, but how do you feel about others who are not punctual?

How do you treat people when they are late?

And what happens with you when you are unable to be on time?

Or perhaps

you're the

person who

never seems

to be on time.

Do you know how you manage to do that?

What are the steps you take that make you late most of the time?

What do you believe about yourself as a person who is late?

What do the voices in your head say about you?

What do you project others think about you?

EXERCISE

To see more clearly, take a few
moments and record what you see about
your relationship with time.

Record what the voices are saying to you,
what is being projected,
what self-hating messages are being
delivered,
the two bad choices you are being given.

Listen to the recording and see if you can
articulate the process of suffering and
identity maintenance that
goes on for you regarding
time management.

Perhaps you're hearing voices (probably calm, logical voices) letting you know that you really don't have time for this kind of stuff. Introspection is good and helpful, of course, but there just isn't time right now. Maybe later when... the kids are grown? you've retired? you've died of old age?

The truth is, you can't afford NOT to "waste time" on this kind of stuff!!!

Conditioning is working hard
to ruin your life.
You must work at least as hard
not to let it.

The rewards are enormous.

Note: You could start by using time-management as the focus of the 30-day retreat at the back of the book.

9. Self-Discipline vs. Self-Improvement

Compassionate self-discipline has nothing to do with self-improvement.

Self-improvement comes from conditioning you received as a child, is based on a false premise that there is something wrong with you, and results in suffering.
Zen is a path of ending suffering.

People try to "fix" us when we are children. Their motives might be good - they want us to be safe and socially acceptable (it's what was done to them) - and now, as adults, we've taken on the job ourselves. But just because that happened, doesn't mean it has to continue.

So much of what passes for education is nothing more than adults inflicting their unexamined beliefs and assumptions onto children and projecting their own unexamined reasons and motivations onto children's reactions. Parents often forget that children do not know what the parents know, have not had the experience the parents have had. For instance, children don't understand what money is or what it means or how stressful it can be for adults to get and keep enough money. Children don't have bills or hold jobs or worry about old age or retirement. In fact, it's quite a while before children know that money doesn't grow on trees. Bananas do. Why not money?

For a child the world is a huge unknown. Every aspect of life is brand new. (It is for each of us, but as adults we've mostly forgotten this.) Instead of a parent or teacher taking a step-by-step approach to "the how of learning," most children get the stumble-through-and-figure-it-out-for-yourself-in-pain-and-suffering approach.

"I have already told you that!" means little to a child confronting a vast array of new information with no clues about what is important to focus on. "I have already told you that!" means there is something wrong with you that you need to fix! Once we buy into the belief that mistakes are possible, that who we are and what we do is "wrong," we become afraid of asking questions. We internalize not asking for clarification or support as the good/right person way to be. If we get yelled at repeatedly for being curious, there is no reason to explore and learn. When the focus is on what's wrong, the focus is not on what's there to learn.

Some years ago while guiding some workshops at an outdoor center I was invited to learn to kayak. Now, I'm not overly fond of water and would never have approached kayaking of my own volition, but since I began teaching awareness practice—a natural love of mine—I have made it a practice to take up new activities, usually physical, that are not easy for me so I can stay in touch with what it's like to learn new, potentially scary stuff.

So, there we were, sitting in an eddy, reading the river (which was utterly lost on me), and getting ready to paddle across to the other side. My instructor, a world-class whitewater competitor and

instructor
(yes, she was
in the
Olympics)
began taking
me through
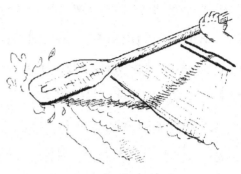
all the information I would need to get
from here to there. Okay, okay, yeah,
okay, got it. Ready? My head is nodding yes
while every muscle in my body has locked
into NO.

Divine intervention must have kept me in
that little boat because my performance
was something less than stellar. I got
several more tips. The next trip was
worse.

Finally, as we pulled into another eddy and
I pantingly got my little craft turned in
the right direction, I asked my teacher to
tell me the three most important things
to know in this moment. I realized there
was no context into which I could

integrate theory or philosophy or contingency plans. I needed one place to focus my attention and two other places to be aware of. That's all! As I mastered those I could sense the next step as she offered it, and then the next.

This is compassion in action!

At the Zen Monastery Peace Center, when a person arrives for a period of monastic training, they are immediately given a  job outside their area of expertise. They are asked to do this task in a very specific way and are guided to perform the task precisely as requested. They are closely supervised and allowed no independent decisions, what we call "better ideas." This accomplishes several marvelous objectives once the person moves past the horror of feeling about three years old in a grown-up world.

--The student does not have to be smart, clever, knowledgeable, or a high achiever.

--The student can let go of all other concerns and simply be present to a simple task.

--The student gets to see and hear all the conditioning that is in the way of being present in the moment.

--The student gets to move out of the head and into the body.

--And most important of all, the student gets to learn how to learn.

The Monastery exists because it is critical that this transformative work happen in a safe, "privileged" environment. As the student practices, usually feeling like a small child, hearing the voices of conditioned fear, anger, judgment, and self-hatred, they are encouraged to Record and Listen. Through conversations with the Mentor, they train to disidentify from their conditioned orientation of self-improvement and rediscover their love of learning.

In the present, we can undo the past and release the future through bringing conscious, compassionate awareness to that in us that suffers. The specific process of ending suffering from the past is to embrace in compassion what was injured by unconscious conditioning. Consciously acknowledging the identification with an experience from the past enables us to move into the present, into acceptance and kindness.

10. Awareness Practice

We call this work "awareness practice." Awareness practice unveils that which keeps us from a natural state of ease and acceptance and joy. We bring the assumptions, lies, illusions, and fantasies of conditioned mind into the light, revealing the delusions that run our lives, that imprison us in suffering.

As you begin the "30 Days of Compassionate Self-Discipline" retreat, remember that the point is not to succeed or fail, not to be a good person for doing it right or a bad person for doing it wrong, but just to see what happens, to reveal how suffering is caused by our relationship with conditioned mind and in that awareness make the choice to end suffering.

Guided Retreat

30 Days of Compassionate Self-Discipline

This 30-day guided retreat is basic training in awareness practice.

You will choose an aspect of your life in which you identify the problem to be self-discipline. In doing the daily exercises, you will be guided to see the conditioned process that interferes with your ability to be present.

As you do these
daily exercises and practices,
you will learn how to pay attention.

You will develop the ability to turn attention to any aspect of life and see how conditioned patterns are keeping you from being present. You will learn to turn to presence for encouragement, assistance, and support to make the changes you want for your life.

You need a recording device and a journal for this retreat.

An Encouragement:

You might quit this program
a hundred times
before you finish it.
That's not a problem.

In fact, that would be a good thing. Quit and then recommit as soon as you realize you've quit. Do the exercises each time you recommit and your ability to pay attention and your understanding will expand.

You could start this guided retreat at the beginning of the month, complete it, and start again at the beginning of the next month *for the rest of your life* and your life would be completely transformed.

So whenever the voices talk you into quitting, notice everything about how that happens: what they say, what you believe, how you feel, what happens in your body, what choices you make while under the direction and influence of the voices. Then start the retreat at Day 1 as soon as you wake up and realize what happened.

DAY 1

Choose a personal problem or concern with which to practice compassionate self-discipline for this guided retreat. We are practicing with PROCESS; the CONTENT is largely irrelevant.

Examples of "content": junk food, alcohol, exercise, children, spouse, work, procrastination, punctuality, stress, emotions, temper, responsibility, money, sex, control, saying no, guilt, fear, anxiety, gluttony, etc.

Choose something that is not your biggest issue. Practicing with less charged content can help us see the same conditioned processes that dictate our quality of life with the big issues. If you have difficulty exercising, but much more difficulty with junk food, choose exercising. If alcohol is a huge issue, but you procrastinate daily, pick procrastination. It's easier to see the self-hating process when we have fewer beliefs about the importance of the issue. Because we are working with a process, you will be able to apply the principles to any content in your life.

Jot down the "problem."

DAY 2

Explore why you want to work with this particular issue. What do you really want to address? If you are successful, what will you have? R/L

DAY 3

For the next 24 hours, get as comprehensive a picture as you can of what you hear in your head about this issue. Keep the issue in the front of your awareness as you go about your day. Each time you become aware that attention is on the issue, notice what the voices are saying and jot it down.

DAY 4

Notice how much of the conversation in your head is in support of unexamined beliefs and assumptions.

Review the statements from the voices that you jotted down. What beliefs and assumptions are revealed? A belief or assumption can be revealed by a single statement or a collection of statements. Write down the beliefs and assumptions. R/L what you see.

Example:
The voices say I don't have time to exercise.
The belief is that my responsibilities are more important than what takes care of me.

DAY 5

Before a fair amount of introspection reveals something different, we believe that we are a single, unified entity. I'm me. "I" am "me." I think my thoughts and feel my feelings. Upon closer examination, we begin to notice there is more than one "I" making up "me."

Review the conversation you jotted down about this issue and begin to identify the various "I's" having the conversation. One way to do this is to group similar statements. Find a word or phrase that describes each "I." It's likely to be a quality or characteristic.
R/L what you see.

Here are examples:

The voices:

I don't have time to exercise.
I have to get X, Y, Z done today.
Other people clearly have more time than I do.
I'm too busy.
It's my job.

The "I's":

"Responsible"
It's my job.
What I have to get done today is X, Y, Z

"Victim"
Other people clearly have more time than I do.

"Stressed"
I don't have time to exercise. I'm too busy.

DAY 6

Our definition of an aspect of the personality is a collection of beliefs, assumptions and projections, holding a unique world view and distinct language.

With that in mind, consider the descriptors from the previous assignment and begin to flesh out the "I's" such that you can recognize each as a separate "personality" with its own worldview. Write down the language each uses and what each projects onto others, the world, and "you." R/L what you see.

As you work with this, make sure to stay on topic, confining the exploration to the specifics of what you are looking at this month.

Example:
Stressed's worldview, language, and projections are "It's too hard. It's overwhelming. I can't do this. It's always been this way. It's always going to be this way. I can't stand it. My body is tense and tight. I feel irritable and angry."

DAY 7

Draw portraits of the aspects of the
personality you have seen. Jot down what
each says. R/L

DAY 8

Go back and review the conversation in your head that you have jotted down about this issue to see if there are any voices you've not captured.

Example
Voice missing: I really *want* to exercise.
Voice missing: You *should* exercise.

R/L what you see.

DAY 9

Is there a duality operating that you can identify?

Rearrange the voices on two sides of the duality. Which aspect of the personality do you see on each side? R/L

Example
One side: I should exercise. (Responsible)
Second Side: I've got too much
to do to exercise. (Stressed)

DAY 10

Can you see how the voices are framing your choices to ensure that you never win?

Example
If I exercise, I'm not being responsible because I'm not doing what I should be doing. If I'm doing what I should be doing, I'm not exercising, which is also what I should be doing. Either way I feel bad!

What are the two choices the voices offer you?

R/L what you see

DAY 11

What possibilities might be available if you dropped out of the either/or framing of the issue?

R/L what you see.

DAY 12

There's a good chance that with all of this paying attention to the voices in your head you are finding yourself able to distinguish self-hating voices. Name-calling, shaming, blaming, cruel statements about who and how you are - the kinds of things you would never say to or about someone you care about - are examples of self-hatred.

What self-hating voices do you hear about this issue? Write down the self-hating messages.

Example
You're not exercising.
You're out of shape. You'll get fat.

Note: Never record self-hating messages.

DAY 13

There is always an implied message underlying what self-hate says. Like the raised eyebrow that is loaded with meaning, every self-hating voice is loaded with implications.

What message about who or how you are is being implied by the self-hating messages?

Example
The underlying message in "You'll be out of shape and unfit" is "You are not lovable as you are. You have to look good to be loved."

R/L what you see.

DAY 14

The self-hating message is that as we are, we are not enough.

Enough for what?
What does that mean?
If you were "enough," then what?

R/L what you see.

DAY 15

As you read over how suffering happens for you, can you get a sense of the conditioning behind this issue? What beliefs, assumptions, projections and behaviors do you consistently choose that result in suffering?

Example
The good-and-right person thing to do is to be responsible. Above all else I must be responsible.
That's the conditioned choice I make over exercising.

R/L what you see.

DAY 16

This whole suffering process is set up to keep the conditioning in place.

"I have to meet certain standards that fix or change me, that make me better, the way I *should* be to be acceptable and lovable. Yet, meeting those standards doesn't get me the acceptance and love that I have assumed I will receive if I meet the standards."

This orientation misses the point, entirely. We are being conned into believing that our "Inherent Goodness" is conditional. It assumes that Authentic Nature is dependent upon performance. So, attention is taken away from our

Authentic Nature and turned to an identity maintaining dualistic conversation that causes us to believe our acceptance is conditional.

Make a recording that reminds you of what is true about you that will support you not to fall for and be tortured by the lies of a self-hating voice.

Listen to and add to your recordings as you get clearer about what is true about you.

DAY 17

We are conditioned to be a human sacrifice.
We are sacrificed to maintain the conditioning.

Example
I love to be outside, to move, to be physical, to play, and to be engaged with life, but this is not allowed.
I am too busy and have too much to do for any of that.

What of you is sacrificed when the conditioning is chosen? R/L what you see.

DAY 18

The Buddha taught that we each have one life to save—our own. We are each capable of being the conscious, compassionate awareness that ends suffering. Compassionate self-discipline is a big part of the "how" of ending suffering.

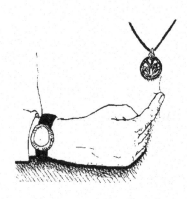

What would you have to let go of, surrender, and lose interest in for the suffering not to be maintained?

The obvious answer is the voices, but see if you can go beyond the obvious.

R/L what you see.

DAY 19

The conversation in conditioned mind often holds the key to the issue I'm facing. However, the way the conversation is framed causes the attention to go to what is *not so* rather than what *is so*.

Example
The voices say that I have to be responsible and get my work done. But some days if I do my work I don't have time to exercise. The implication is that being responsible means working and precludes everything else. When I stop and consider this, I can explore what I truly want to be responsible for and to.

I want to be responsible not just for doing my job but for my well-being. I can

do the work I am called to do and also
take care of my body.

What is the answer that is
revealed to you by the
conversation?

R/L what you see.

DAY 20

Eventually, we realize that the suffering in any content area is caused by egocentric karmic conditioning/self-hate, not the content.

As a one-week practice, choose a behavior change, not a content change, that addresses the process you've discovered in the retreat so far. Make sure you choose something that can be practiced for a week.

Example
Let's say I am working with "I'm not disciplined about exercise." The issue is framed for me as "I don't have time to exercise." But in this retreat I have seen that my conditioned definition of responsible precludes everything other than work. And so my conditioning

regarding being responsible is really the process I will work with. My realization is that it's not true that I have to choose between work and exercise. The behavior change I will practice is to be responsible by doing the work that is mine to do and taking care of myself by exercising.

Another Example

If I feel deprived that I cannot have all the carbohydrates I want, I don't want to make a commitment not to eat sugar. My behavior change is to take on the *process of deprivation* as the issue and make choices every day that help me feel satisfied, given to, and grateful.

Make a commitment poster that states your behavior change.

Make a recording that
1) refutes the self-hating messages
2) replaces the conditioned conversation with what you choose instead.

DAY 21

Beginning today, your **Daily Practice** will be to:

1. Start your day by listening to your recording from Day 20.
2. Practice your behavior change.
3. Record what you notice at the end of the day.

DAY 22

Do your **Daily Practice** - whether you feel like it or not!

Practice ignoring any voice of resistance, especially
"I don't want to and I don't feel like it."

Remember:
Willingness is what's there when we don't want to. Willingness is not will power. As you have no doubt realized throughout a lifetime of resolutions and self-improvement projects, willpower lacks staying power. We can get inspired and fired up to make some sort of change, and in a shockingly short time run out of steam. Once you comprehend compassionate

self-discipline, you will no longer have to rely on inspiration or willpower to accomplish what you want to accomplish. You will have more than tools and techniques to make changes or obtain results; you will have an attitude of mind and heart that makes just about anything in life available to you.

DAY 23

Do your **Daily Practice,** being on the lookout for any subtle messages of self-hate.

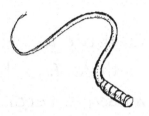

Use any negative message as a reminder to redirect attention to what is true about you.

R/L what you notice.

DAY 24

Do your **Daily Practice.**

Cultivate an encouraging, supportive attitude. Each time you hear a negative message, record an encouraging message to the person doing this work.

Encouragement

We're not always identified with an aspect of our self who **wants to.** That's not a problem as long as we're **willing.** I may not want to get up three times in the night with the baby, but I'm willing to. I am willing because who I really am (conscious, compassionate awareness) is bigger than any aspect of the personality who has slipped into the driver's seat of my life at the moment of choice.

DAY 25

Do your **Daily Practice.**

Negative voices want you to focus on
what's not working. As you go about your
day, notice all the things that are working.
Notice how adequate you are to your life
experience. R/L

DAY 26

Do your **Daily Practice.**

If you are willing to consider that punishment is not what makes people good, and that it contributes to self-hating choices, come up with a special way to express appreciation for the practitioner (you). What method of appreciation will replace the self-hate, judgment, and punishment that conditioning uses to control you? What makes you feel appreciated? What makes you feel loved? When you do a good job, what do you want to hear? What do you say to those you care about that shows your appreciation?

Record a letter of appreciation and listen to it.

Remember, appreciation is not related to performance. We are practicing Unconditional Love and Acceptance.

DAY 27

Do your **Daily Practice.**

Focus on kindness today, all the kindness
you receive and all the
kindness you offer.

DAY 28

Do your **Daily Practice.**

Today, focus on gratitude for what you have.

DAY 29

Do your **Daily Practice.**

Make a recording that captures what you've learned from working with this month's content focus. Perhaps start a folder that allows easy access for review.

To jog your memory: In the past 30 days, you've been training in compassionate self-discipline. Instead of being caught in the trap of having failed because of a lack of self-discipline, you've been practicing seeing and seeing through what keeps you from being present and able to keep your commitments.

You've brought awareness to the conversation in conditioned mind about this content, worked with aspects of the personality, questioned conditioned beliefs, identified self-hating messages, and seen the dualities and the conditioning being maintained. You've worked with conscious, compassionate awareness on the behavior change that will help you exit suffering and make the choices that take care of you. And, hopefully, you've learned that kindness will take you to places punishment never could.

DAY 30

Do your **Daily Practice.**

Decide how to celebrate the completion of this round of your compassionate self-discipline retreat. Will you celebrate alone? Will you invite a friend or partner? Would you like to have a whole crowd to celebrate with? Will you tell others about your accomplishment?

Have that celebration and don't forget to make a celebration recording!

The components of a happy life:
appreciation, gratitude, kindness,
willingness, love, and
compassionate awareness.

I will not abandon
myself no
matter what.

I will ask for
help if I
need it.

Deep down
this is what
I really want.

I know I cannot
fail if I do this
with love.

Conditioning, self-hatred, worry, the
voices, the stories, fear, anxiety, past
and future concerns, urgency, loss, lack,
deprivation, "something wrong," and "not
enough" contribute nothing that will lead
to a happy life. Nothing. They are just
useless.

So Make a Change for Good by
committing to practicing the components
of a happy life. Repeat this retreat with

other areas of life where the voices say you need more discipline and bring conscious compassionate awareness to those areas as well.

Come up with your next commitment and begin again at Day 1.

WELL DONE!
CONGRATULATIONS!

Work with Cheri Huber

To talk with Cheri call in to Open Air, her internet-based radio show. Archives of the show and instructions on how to participate are available at www.openairwithcherihuber.org.

To work with Cheri on an individual basis, sign up for her email classes at livingcompassion.org/schedule.

Visit www.recordingandlistening.org to learn about Recording and Listening, the practice that is Cheri's passion.

Visit cherihuber.com to access Cheri's latest interviews.

Cheri's books are available from your local independent bookstore, www.keepitsimple.org, and other online booksellers.

A Center for the Practice
of Zen Buddhist Meditation

Visit livingcompassion.org for more information on Zen Awareness Practice and the teachings of Cheri Huber.

- Find a schedule of retreats and workshops
- Find out more about virtual practice opportunities such as Reflective Listening, Virtual Meditation and Email Classes
- Access newsletters and blogs on Zen Awareness Practice
- Sign up for Recording and Listening Training
- Find out about our work in a community in Zambia. Read blogs with updates.

Contact

information@livingcompassion.org

There Is Nothing Wrong with You

An Extraordinary Eight-Day Retreat
based on the book
*There Is Nothing Wrong with You:
Going Beyond Self-Hate*
by Cheri Huber

Inside each of us is a "persistent voice of discontent." It is constantly critical of life, the world, and almost everything we say and do. As children, in order to survive we learned to listen to this voice and believe what it says.

This retreat is eight days of looking directly at how we are rejected and punished by the voices of self-hate and discovering how to let that go. Through a variety of exercises and periods of group processing, participants gain a clearer perspective on how they live their lives and on how to find compassion for themselves and others.

This work is challenging, joyous, fulfilling, scary, courageous, demanding, freeing, loving, kind, and compassionate— compassionate toward yourself and everyone you will ever know.

For information on attending, contact:
information@livingcompassion.org

What Universe Are You Creating? is a playful, powerful way to learn the skill of Recording and Listening, a revolutionary tool for practicing turning attention from incessant, haranguing, karmically conditioned patterns of thought and action to the peace of presence. Recording in your own voice and then listening to kind words, encouragement, inspirational readings, favorite songs, gratitude lists, meditations—in short, being your own mentor—turns attention away from the constant stream of negative self-talk, robbing it of its power by revealing its illusory nature. ISBN: 9780991596300